YOUR KNOWLEDGE HAS VALUE

Amritpal Hayre

Business Strategy of British Airways. A Case Study

GRIN Publishing

Bibliographic information published by the German National Library:

The German National Library lists this publication in the National Bibliography; detailed bibliographic data are available on the Internet at http://dnb.dnb.de .

Imprint:

Copyright © 2014 GRIN Verlag GmbH
Print and binding: Books on Demand GmbH, Norderstedt Germany
ISBN: 978-3-656-87562-8

This book at GRIN:

http://www.grin.com/en/e-book/287089/business-strategy-of-british-airways-a-case-study

GRIN - Your knowledge has value

Since its foundation in 1998, GRIN has specialized in publishing academic texts by students, college teachers and other academics as e-book and printed book. The website www.grin.com is an ideal platform for presenting term papers, final papers, scientific essays, dissertations and specialist books.

Visit us on the internet:

http://www.grin.com/

http://www.facebook.com/grincom

http://www.twitter.com/grin_com

Case Study: British Airways

By: Amritpal Singh Hayre

Table of Contents

1.   Introduction

In this assignment I will discuss British Airways in a strategic context whilst producing organisational and environmental audits. Furthermore I will identify the stakeholders and choose a business strategy. Finally I will propose timescales to achieve and monitor the strategy whilst identifying the resource requirements.

2.   Strategic Context

British Airways (BA) is the UK's flagship airline which on a daily basis provides flights to over 400 cities globally. The vision statement of the company as stated by British Airways (2007) is 'become the World's most responsible Airline'. An objective is the result a business wants to achieve within a specific period of time. The company does not possess a mission statement or an objective however it does have a philosophy which is 'to be the world's global premium airline' as stated in British Airways (2008).

A goal is a purpose toward which a venture is concentrated upon. The goals of the company as stated in British Airways (2008) are to 'be the airline of choice for long-haul premium customers' and 'meet customers' needs and improve margins through new revenue streams'.

The core competency of a business is the major potencies and benefits which it possesses such as knowledge and resources. The core competencies of BA are providing a premium quality service and providing flights to every major city in the world which has lead them to being the UK's major market share holder as stated by Romanova (2005).

3.   Strategic Planning Issues

An issue in strategic planning which may impact BA is the internal resources of the company. For instance if the company's plane's jets have become low in quality and Boeing only produces one type of jet then BA would have to find an alternative supplier. Therefore the company would have to research on alternative suppliers and decide on the best price for quality and decide on how much of the jets are required and how long it would take to attach the jets to their existing fleet.

Another issue in strategic planning is the individuals who should be involved. For example if BA decides to introduce a new business strategy then they must decide who should be involved in the planning of the strategy. May (2010) suggests to decide on who should be involved would take a lot of time since the company must decide what departments will be impacted by the new strategy and who would be able to implement the strategy.

The final issue of strategic planning is the external environment. This is an issue due to the fact that the external environment is volatile and is affected by extreme variables. For instance if BA have carried out research on the market determining that the current prices are adequate enough to generate their interest and decide to keep them but suddenly a rise in tax has been announced and the market want to purchase budget airline tickets then the research must be carried out again as to how much they are willing to spend and what methods can BA use to cut their prices.

4. Planning Techniques

A planning technique which can be applied is the BCG Growth-Share Matrix. Daft (2008) states this method enables an organisation to allocate resources whilst analysing its market position to decide an appropriate strategy to improve or maintain operations.

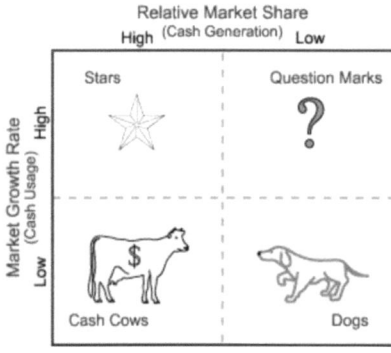

Figure 1 by QuickMBA (2010)

The planning technique in figure 1 can be used by BA to determine what the current position of the business is in terms of their market share and their market growth rate. For BA in the UK's aviation market it is a Cash Cow since it constitutes the majority of the market share however the growth rate is minimal since the market is beginning to saturate with low-cost companies entering i.e. EasyJet. The ideal thing to do in this situation is to use the 'hold' strategy meaning the company attempts to maintain its current position and generate high sums of money as it currently is doing.

Another planning technique which can be applied is the Strategic Position and Action Evaluation (SPACE). Thompson (2011) suggests this technique is similar to the Growth-Share Matrix since it positions a company based on its financial and industry strength, environmental stability, and competitive advantage.

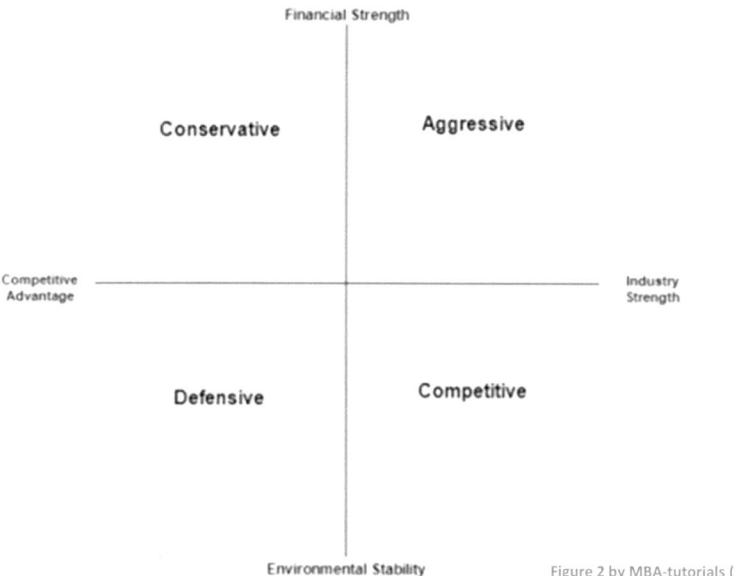

Figure 2 by MBA-tutorials (2010)

The positioning of BA in the SPACE matrix would lead the business to adopt an 'aggressive' strategy. This is because the company has sufficient financial strength to invest in new innovative projects so they can maintain and sustain a competitive advantage furthermore reducing prices to such levels that it would be impossible for rivals to compete with. Also since the company is using an aggressive strategy then it should start to buying-out rivals and smaller competitors thus enabling BA to be the market dominator and building barriers for entry and exit which means fewer companies enter the market and companies that want to leave can be bought-out by BA.

5.   Organisational Audit

The organisational audit of British Airways observes the company's existing circumstances such as their resources which are financial, human, physical, and intellectual capital.

In terms of BA their physical resources are their aircraft fleet and any facility on board the planes. The material input is the supplier of the planes which would be Boeing and Airbus. As of 2013 the company has a total fleet of 270 aircrafts whilst 76 have been ordered for the future; the fleet is accessible world-wide since they travel to over 200 destinations in the world and operate at all the major airports.

The Human Resources of BA are their staff and their knowledge and skills regarding their jobs. BA has roughly 57,000 employees which amount for £2.3 billion in costs as shown in British Airways (2012). Each individual has their own skill from the pilots who operate the planes to the sales assistants at the check-in counter thus everyone is a 'valuable asset' since without their own skills and knowledge the company would not be able to operate effectively.

The financial resources of BA are their fixed assets, working capital and short/long-term finances. The fixed assets amount to £6.5 billion as shown in British Airways (2012) with a net gearing ratio of 63.46 and a net working capital of -£1.06 billion as presented by ADVFN (2013).

The intellectual capital of BA is their patents, brand, and relationships with customers. Patentdocs (2013) states he company has 4 patents regarding the seating units on their aircrafts and how they are able to recline and form a sleeping position. The brand has its own trademark logo which enables customers to differentiate BA from other airlines. And the relationship with customers is built on trust by providing a premium service to customers and financial compensation if a flight is cancelled or unsatisfactory.

6.   Environmental Audit

The environmental audit of British Airways observes the environmental performance and position of the company.

The strategy which is used by BA in terms of the environment is to conduct an analysis which identifies various methods the business is able to execute in order to reduce its carbon footprint. An initiative which the company has introduced is the 'one destination carbon fund' this is a non-profit entity in which customers donate money for BA to help provide renewable energy to the local community.

One Destination (2012) states that the initiative has seen a solar swimming pool installed at a local swimming pool in Newcastle, a biomass boiler at a leisure centre in Cornwall, and the introduction of solar panels at a leisure centre in Weymouth.

Furthermore British Airways (2008) states that it has recycled 35% of the waste the company produces at both Heathrow and Gatwick whilst the amount of waste sent to the landfill sites in Heathrow was reduced by 7.2%. Also the company has begun a long-term 'carbon efficiency programme' to reduce its emissions; in 2009 BA produced C02 emissions of 106.1 per km in comparison to an average car which was 109 per km whilst the carbon footprint of the business was 16.7m tonnes (a 5.2% reduction from the previous year) as stated by British Airways (2009).

	Target	2009*	2008*	2007
Carbon efficiency gCO2/pkm**	83 by 2025	106	107	110
CO2 emission (million tonnes)		16.67	17.60	17.7
Average noise per flight	15% reduction by 2015	On track***	On track***	On track***
% Recycling (LHR and LGW)	50% by end 2010	39.0	35.1	30.1
Waste to landfill (tonnes LHR and LGW)	zero to landfill by end of 2010	2,187	3,424	3,688

*Calendar years.

Figure 3 by British Airways (2009)

Figure 3 shows the progress BA has made between the period of 2007 – 2009 and the long-term targets are for the organisation regarding each environmental situation. As the table clearly shows that in the entire environment sectors the company has seen a reduction in its excess waste and a rise in the % it has recycled over the 3 year period.

7.   Stakeholders

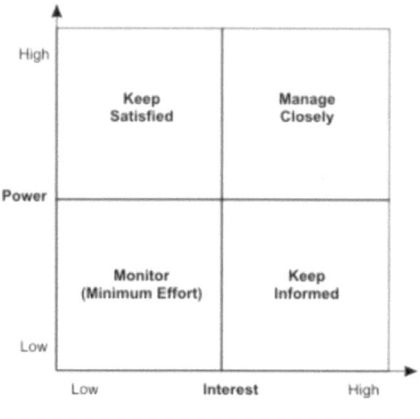

Figure 5 by Mind Tools (2013)

The key stakeholders are customers, employees, suppliers, and shareholders. Figure 4 indicates customers are 'keep satisfied' stakeholders since they are the target audience and expect a 'quality service' thus BA strives to meet their needs. The employees are also 'keep satisfied' since their job security is paramount thus BA must consider the impact any expansion or contraction has on them. Suppliers are in the 'keep informed' category because they provide aircrafts which is the main product of the company and if BA is performing well then the suppliers would see more demand in their goods. The shareholders are 'manage closely' since they aim to see a return on their investment thus any strategies implemented must consider the profitability of the operation.

Schwalbe (2008) states stakeholder analysis is vital for organisations due to the fact that they are able to familiarize themselves with the needs of their stakeholders. Furthermore businesses can identify the impact an action has on stakeholders and thus they can decide whether there are any risks involved with executing that action. Patel (2004) suggests through this method businesses can decide which stakeholders are 'more important' than others as well as identifying methods and strategies to persuade stakeholders to support an action whilst reducing the risk by preventing conflicts of interest.

An opportunity which BA is facing is the chance of making an eco-friendly travel method thus ensuring the company is not impacting the environment too much. The second opportunity BA has is to invest in its aircrafts to provide better quality seating for their customers since they own a couple of patents. The problems which BA faces are budget airlines entering the market thus reducing the market share of BA and new entrants offering lower prices which BA is unable to compete with.

8.   Alternative Strategies

An alternative strategy BA can use for substantive growth is horizontal integration. Hill and Jones (2012) suggest this is a method where a business acquires supplementary activities from either parallel or dissimilar industries which are in the same phase of production thus permitting sharing resources. Through the use of this strategy BA can purchase aircraft suppliers thus allowing them to produce aircrafts whilst developing other facilities which they can help differentiate their service from their rivals. Thus BA maintains its dominance since it does not rely on suppliers for aircrafts; meaning if the company wants to modify its airlines then they can do so promptly.

Another strategy BA can use is market development for limited growth. Hodge (2006) states this is where a business expands its market through transferring non-buyers to customers as well as introducing new segments to the market. Since British Airways is not popular in countries like China and India (population over a billion each) therefore BA can attempt to enter these untapped markets to provide domestic travel and attract new customers. Since many businessmen and individuals have families and companies situated all over their respective country thus they will have a demand for BA's product since they provide a luxury service for domestic flights.

The final strategy BA can use is to divest for retrenchment. Povaly (2007) declares this is when a business begins to sell its assets which may be because of an adjustment in corporate strategy or the social goals of the company. British Airways can start to sell of its larger aircrafts which are used for flights that are over 6 hours thus the business can focus on providing flights within Europe instead of globally. Through the sale of the larger aircrafts BA can retain the capital and focus on buying smaller aircrafts for its market as well as heavily promoting the airline in Europe.

9.   Horizontal Integration

The stratagem I have chosen for BA to pursue is Horizontal Integration. This is because it enables the company to become 'innovative' in terms of modifying their aircrafts themselves so they can meet the expectations of their market who do not have a brand loyalty as they usually look for the best facility and price for their flights. Katie (2013) suggests through this method companies are able to increase their powers within the market in other words reduce the bargaining power of external customers like buyers and suppliers.

Furthermore since this business strategy offers British Airways the opportunity to produce aircrafts then the business can actually start providing their own manufactured aeroplanes to other airlines thus enabling the company to gain a foothold in the manufacturing industry since they are an airline company that know what the market wants instead of companies informing the manufacturer what the airline needs to have. Therefore British Airways have another source of income which can be extracted from their innovation and manufacturing business if they implement this strategy.

However if British Airways does not want to sell their manufactured aircrafts and want to keep them for themselves then that would help the business gain a higher market share. This is due to the fact that since BA can conduct research on their customers and what their interests and needs are they can produce an 'appropriate' plane for them whilst bearing in mind the cost to produce it; thus BA's aeroplanes will meet the needs of the market whilst only being exclusively available to their customers. Additionally as BA will be the only airline that manufactures its own aircrafts then they can set-up barriers to entry thus preventing companies like Virgin Atlantic from copying their strategy and sharing the market with them.

10. Resource Requirements

A resource which is required to implement my suggested strategy would be human resources. Randhawa (2007) suggests human resources are an integral part of a business since they aim to meet the business' aims and objectives which had lead companies to treat HR as assets. The man-power required for producing the aircrafts need to be experienced and experts therefore BA must employ full-time workers that can produce aircrafts as well as come-up with innovative ideas. Furthermore the director of BA is required in order to set-out the timeframe and process to employ the strategy and begin operating the strategy.

The second resource the business requires is physical resources. Marinel (2005) states a physical resource is vital for a business because it permits them to operate effectively. A type of physical resource required for this strategy would be machinery which would permit the workers to produce the aircrafts at an equivalent quality of Boeing and Airbus. Another physical resource is having production factories so that BA can produce the aircrafts near the airports and once completed they can be used immediately after passing the health and safety tests.

The final resource which is required to implement the strategy is finance. Damodaran (2010) states finance is an important instrument for businesses as it permits them to spend on resources and assets to execute their functions effectively. BA must invest considerable sums of money to purchase the physical resources for the business strategy as well as employing workers for producing the aircrafts. Thus the organisation can sell shares of their aircraft production business on the stock exchange to generate income to invest into the business; permitting BA to spend a minimal amount for the start-up cost of the new business.

11.   Targets and Timescales

The targets which the business can introduce is on a monthly basis evaluate how many aircrafts have been produced to decide whether the production factories and the workers are meeting the time requirements. Through the use of this method British Airways can surmise whether they are able to cope with the demand for their airlines and decide whether to acquire more production factories for the future to meet the demand of the customers.

Furthermore a long-term target which the company can set is to see an increase in market share by 5% in 4 years. This target can be broken down into smaller target by evaluating on annual basis how much their market share is and how much money the new business strategy is generating. Therefore it allows the business to modify its operations in order to keep on track to meet their long-term and short-term aims and objectives.

An example of a timescale for British Airways' new strategy would be the following:

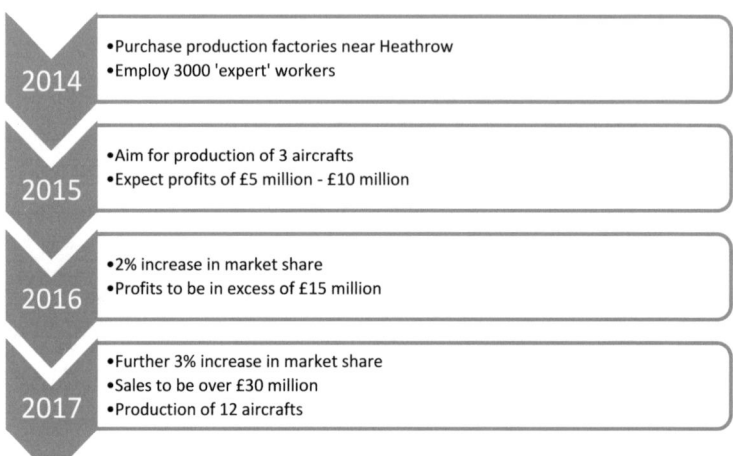

2014
- Purchase production factories near Heathrow
- Employ 3000 'expert' workers

2015
- Aim for production of 3 aircrafts
- Expect profits of £5 million - £10 million

2016
- 2% increase in market share
- Profits to be in excess of £15 million

2017
- Further 3% increase in market share
- Sales to be over £30 million
- Production of 12 aircrafts

The main factor which British Airways must analyse to monitor the business strategy is the key performance indicators of their aircraft production venture. The key performance indicators for the business would be the amount of aircrafts the company produces on annual basis, the number of customers, profit generated, and the % in market share.

Through these key performance indicators the organisation is able to monitor the behaviour of the market and deduce whether the strategy is performing as expected; and if not what changes must be executed to achieve the strategy i.e. make staff redundant to lower costs or sell at a cheaper price to increase demand etc.

12. Conclusion

In conclusion I believe that choosing a strategy for a business like British Airways will take considerable time and money to evaluate every option for the business to ensure it meets its long-term and short-term aims. Therefore using the BCG Growth-Share Matrix and SPACE matrix along with an environmental and organisational audit will aid the business to choose the appropriate strategy whilst considering the key stakeholders who will be impacted by the strategic change.

Furthermore the implementation of a business strategy must be monitored continually to ensure the organisation is fulfilling its aims and objectives whilst correctly utilizing the resources at hand to apply the strategy. And with suitable targets and time-plans set-up businesses are able to identify the areas which the company is excelling in to attain its goals as well as the areas it must improve thus enabling the company to meet its long-term objectives.

Bibliography

ADVFN. (2013). *British Airways Company Financial Information.* [Online] Available from: <http://www.advfn.com/exchanges/LSE/BAY/financials> [Accessed on 26th December 2013].

British Airways. (2007). *Annual Reports and Accounts.* [Online] Available from: <http://www.britishairways.com/cms/global/microsites/ba_reports/pdfs/13_CR_Intro.p df> [Accessed on 24th December 2013].

British Airways. (2008). *Annual Reports and Accounts.* [Online] Available from: < http://www.britishairways.com/cms/global/microsites/ba_reports0809/pdfs/Strategy.p df> [Accessed on 24th December 2013].

British Airways. (2009). *Annual Reports and Accounts.* [Online] Available from: < http://www.britishairways.com/cms/global/microsites/ba_reports0910/our_business/e nvironment.html> [Accessed on 27th December 2013].

British Airways. (2012). *Annual Reports and Accounts for the period ending 31 December 2012.* [Online] Available from: < http://www.google.co.uk/url?sa=t&rct=j&q=&esrc=s&source=web&cd=2&ved=0CDM QFjAB&url=http%3A%2F%2Fphx.corporate-ir.net%2FExternal.File%3Fitem%3DUGFyZW50SUQ9MTc1Njk3fENoaWxkSUQ9LT F8VHlwZT0z%26t%3D1&ei=fCW8UtDUEMOqhQfK8YGACA&usg=AFQjCNFKz38z5 Wr1s5hwxCX_oN16tE2ccA&bvm=bv.58187178,d.d2k> [Accessed on 26th December 2013].

Daft, R.L. (2008). *The New Era of Management.* Mason, USA: Cengage Learning Inc.

Damodaran, A. (2010). *Applied Corporate Finance.* 3rd edition. Chichester: John Wiley and Sons Ltd.

Hill, C. and Jones, G.R. (2012). *Strategic Management – Theory: An Integrated Approach.* 9th edition. Mason, USA: South Western Education Publishing.

Hodge, G.A. (2006). *Privatization and Market Development: Global Movements in Public Policy Ideas.* Cheltenham: Edward Elgar Publishing Ltd.

Katie, J. (2013). *A Report on Horizontal and Vertical Business Integration.* Munich, Germany: GRIN Verlag.

Marinel, A.L. (2005). *Start and Run Your Own Business: The Complete Guide to Setting Up and Managing a Small Business.* 2nd edition. Oxford: How to Books Ltd.

May, G. (2010). *Strategic Planning: Fundamentals for Small Business.* New York, USA: Business Expert Press.

MBA-tutorials. (2010). *Strategic Position and Action Evaluation (SPACE) Matrix.* [Online] Available from: <http://www.mba-tutorials.com/strategy/1151-strategic-position-and-action-evaluation-space-matrix.html> [Accessed on 26th December 2013].

Mind Tools. (2013). *Stakeholder Analysis*. [Online] Available from: <http://www.mindtools.com/pages/article/newPPM_07.htm> [Accessed on 27th December 2013].

One Destination. (2012). *One Destination Carbon Fund*. [Online] Available from: <http://www.onedestination.co.uk/environment/climate-change/one-destination-carbon-fund/> [Accessed on 27th December 2013].

Patel, N. (2004). *Critical Systems Analysis and Design: A Personal Framework Approach*. London: Taylor & Francis Ltd.

Patentdocs. (2013). *British Airways Plc Patent Applications*. [Online] Available from: <http://www.faqs.org/patents/assignee/british-airways-plc/> [Accessed on 26th December 2013].

Povaly, S. (2007). *Private Equity Exits: Divestment Process Management for Leveraged Buyouts*. Berlin, Germany: Springer-Verlag Berlin and Heidelberg GmbH & Co KG.

QuickMBA. (2010). *BCG Growth-Share Matrix*. [Online] Available from: <http://www.quickmba.com/strategy/matrix/bcg/> [Accessed on 26th December 2013].

Randhawa, G. (2007). *Human Resource Management*. New Delhi, India: Atlantic Publishers & Distributors Pvt Ltd.

Romanova, I. (2005). *Air Transport in the UK: Current Trends and Future Scenarios*. USA: Grin Verlag.

Schwalbe, K. (2008). *Introduction to Project Management*. 2nd edition. Boston, USA: Cengage Learning Inc.

Thompson, J.L. (2001). *Understanding Corporate Strategy*. London: Cengage Learning EMEA.